T0207577

BYSTANDERS

How Secondhand Information about
Jesus Could Have Influenced Lives of
Those Who Never Met Him

Dorothy Stone Harmon

WESTBOW
PRESS®
A DIVISION OF THOMAS NELSON
& ZONDERVAN

WestBow Press books may be ordered through booksellers or by contacting:

WestBow Press
A Division of Thomas Nelson & Zondervan
1663 Liberty Drive
Bloomington, IN 47403
www.westbowpress.com
844-714-3454

ISBN: 978-1-6642-0928-2 (sc)
ISBN: 978-1-6642-0927-5 (hc)
ISBN: 978-1-6642-0929-9 (e)

Library of Congress Control Number: 2020920166

Print information available on the last page.

WestBow Press rev. date: 01/12/2021

With love and pride,

to my three children,

Jim, Craig, and Katrina,

and their remarkable families!

God bless!

CONTENTS

Introduction.. ix

Jotham 1
Maria 7
Ezra... 13
Olivia...19
Jacob 25
Ibram 31
Sarai.. 37
Paulus 43
Esther.. 49
Jaron 55
Miriam...61
Haman.. 67
Nazor 73
Claudius.. 81
Dothan 89

A Backward Look... 95
About the Author 99

INTRODUCTION

Would it be blasphemous, irreverent, or even sinful to imagine people who could have heard about Jesus from those who had been present when he was in their vicinity? Could we imagine the reaction of the Bethlehem innkeeper whose wife attended the newborn in their stable? Or that of the sister of the Gadarene demoniac when he returned home in his right mind? Or that of Peter's father-in-law, whose wife was healed while he was away from home? Or how about the mother of the little boy whose lunch Jesus multiplied to feed the crowd?

How might these and other bystanders react to news about Jesus's ministry? As you read these stories, try to imagine yourself in the place of the person about whom you are reading. How might you react if you had been present in each of these circumstances?

At the end of each story, there is a page titled "Think about It" to help you weigh a possible response.

Thank God for the testimony of the people who really did experience being in the presence of Jesus. Read more of these events and others like them—some of the greatest stories ever told, all true stories—in the best book of all, God's Word.

May God's blessings be with you as you read.

Bystanders is a collection of imaginary testimonies of people who heard about Jesus from other people. They could have found out about him through contact with a family member, friend, neighbor, acquaintance, or other similar encounters. Stories are based on scriptural accounts of actual events in Jesus's life.

These testimonies may be used as private devotionals, teaching units, or dramatic readings. Each is designed to point readers to a closer relationship with Christ as they examine the impact he might have had on others.

Included in the materials are the following:

1. Jotham—Bethlehem innkeeper

2. Maria—mother of boy with loaves and fish

3. Ezra—Peter's father-in-law

4. Olivia—friend of the woman caught in adultery

5. Jacob—roofer of the house where the paralytic was healed

6. Ibram—uncle of Bartimaeus

7. Sarai—sister of the crippled woman

8. Paulus—cousin of Zacchaeus

9. Esther—sister of the Gadarene demoniac

10. Jaron—former husband of the Samaritan woman

11. Miriam—neighbor of Mary and Martha

12. Haman—brother of Simon of Cyrene

13. Nazor—father of witness to the crucifixion

14. Claudius—father of a guard at the gravesite

15. Dotham—cousin of Cleopas

JOTHAM

I've got to admit that these last few months have been the strangest—and busiest—time of my life. I've been an innkeeper in Bethlehem for more than thirty years, and I've had some strange things happen, but an incident last year was the strangest of all. Oh, I'm happy to have had so much business! I have to thank our great Caesar for that. He ordered that everyone had to go back to the place of their birth and be counted. He has an eye for business, that one. The citizens were to be registered in the city of their birth, a countrywide census, so that they could be taxed. More money in his pocket, I guess! But I digress.

Every room in my inn was full on that particular night. There were people from all over the country coming into town. Some families came together; some men came alone. My entire staff was on call in twelve-hour shifts just to be sure that every customer had a place to sleep and we had enough provisions to make them comfortable. It was getting rather late when this man who said his name was Joseph came to ask for lodging. He seemed to be quite anxious and—well, I would say—rather desperate. When I asked him why he seemed so disturbed, he told me that his wife was about ready to have a baby, and they needed a place right away. I didn't know what to do at first. I told him that there was no more room in the inn and that there were some other lodging places in town. I really didn't have any available rooms, but I honestly didn't want to turn them away under those circumstances. My wife reminded me that our stable had just been cleaned and that there was plenty of hay stocked for the sheep. It was warm and private, and we could give them a safe place to stay. My assistant said that he would see that they were comfortable. My assistant and wife took Joseph and the lady to the stable and helped them to settle down for the night.

After discussing the situation and hoping that this was the last lodger who would come, my wife and I decided to try to get some rest. It had been a long day, and we were both very tired. The children had already been put to bed and were sleeping peacefully, so we decided to retire for what I hoped would be a good night's rest. I was almost asleep when I woke suddenly to see a brilliant light shining. The moon wasn't even out when I went to bed, so it couldn't be that. I got up and walked outside. You can't imagine what the sky looked like. It was as if a million candles had suddenly been lit, and the whole night sky was ablaze! I went back inside quickly and woke my wife. She, too, was amazed by what she saw in the sky. It looked like a great ball of fire, but after a few minutes of looking at it, we could actually distinguish the shape of a large star! We tried to figure out what was going on but couldn't understand what was causing the mysterious glow. I looked, transfixed by the sight, and listened carefully to try to find a hint somewhere. Then my wife said, "Jotham, I heard a baby cry. I know it was a baby's cry! That woman must have given birth already!" I listened carefully, and I was sure I, too, heard a baby cry. My wife said that she would go down and check to be sure that the woman and the baby were all right. She came back after a while and said that both the woman and her new baby boy were comfortable, that everyone was pleased with the birth of a healthy child, and that our two staff members who remained with them had returned to their posts in the inn.

Later on in the night, I heard a lot of noise outside near the stable. I got up again and went outside. I saw several people; it looked like a group of travelers, but they were gathered around the stable where the young couple had been placed for the night. Again, I thought I heard a baby cry. Maybe those people had heard the cry, too, and wanted to see what was happening.

I decided to walk down to the stable to check on the situation and find out if the couple needed help. When I approached the stable, I realized that the people gathered around were several shepherds from the local farming community. They told me that there had been a strange light in the sky and that—and this is weird—an angel had appeared in the sky and told them to go to find this baby, that this child was going to be the one who was promised of God to be the Savior of his people! I decided not to tell them that I had seen the light too. I wanted to hear more about their vision. They told me how surprised and shocked they were when they saw that glow in the night sky, and they didn't quite understand the angel's coming to them with that kind of a message. They couldn't understand why an angel from heaven would speak to them. They weren't priests or rabbis or even very religious, but here they were, gathered around my stable, talking about that baby boy who was lying in his mother's arms so peacefully. I just shook my head, thanked them for their explanation, and told them to please be as quiet as possible so that my other lodgers didn't wake up. Of course, they didn't do that! They started singing and shouting and carrying on like a crazy mob! They finally left just before dawn, and we settled back in for a little more rest time but not more sleep. We still don't understand what happened that strange night when the baby boy was born in our stable. The couple and their baby stayed with us for three days. We found a small room for them the next day, and when they left, we still wondered about all that we had seen and heard on that strange night.

But that's not quite the end of my story! Several weeks later, a group of prominent rulers—I think there were three, although they may have had more with them—came to the door of my inn and asked for information about that light that shone so brightly the night that baby boy was born. They said that they, too, had seen something strange in the sky and were determined to find out more about it. I think they were prophets or something. Some called them *wise men* because they had been inspired to find the person they referred to as "the King of the Jews." They had gone to Jerusalem, the capital city, to inquire about this event and had asked King Herod about it. He was obviously agitated about news of any other king threatening his power, so he called his advisors together to ask them about these prophecies. They told him that this prophet-king was to be born in Bethlehem of Judea, according to information found in writings of the Hebrew prophet Micah. Herod then told them to go find this so-called king and report back to him. They said that they just wanted to know where to find this boy-king so they could verify his existence and worship him, thus fulfilling the prophecy. So they came to my local inn to get the information. I told them that I had heard that the man called Joseph had rented a small house on the other side of town until his wife—I think he called her Mary—was strong enough to return to their home. I guess they went to find him because I didn't hear anything else about those men.

Now I've had some random thoughts about these incidents. My wife and I have talked about these things a lot over the years. I wish now that I hadn't turned that couple away. I'm sure I could have found room. Joseph looked so downcast when I told him that there was no more room in the inn. My wife and I have both come to the conclusion that the baby boy born in our stable those months ago must have been pretty special with all the attention paid to the events surrounding his birth. Maybe he really was who they said he was—the promised one of God. I don't really know, but I believe that if he really is the special one sent from God, others will come to know him, trust him, and do great things in his name. Maybe I can find out more as time goes by. I know that those parents in my stable that night have someone special in their family. I hope they will tell others about what happened when he was born. Maybe people will understand the story when I tell them what happened. I think I'll wait a while to see how much more I can learn about that baby. He is a special treasure. That's for sure!

Think about It!

1. Consider the Word

Read Matthew 2:1–12; Luke 1:26–38; Luke 2:1–20; John 1:14.

2. Consider Your Response

If you have children or have been close to someone with a newborn, think back to the time of the birth. How did you feel when you heard the first cry or looked at that peaceful little face? How did you feel when you held that little one for the first time? Try to imagine how these two new parents felt. Then try to imagine how they might explain all the attention directed to their child—Jesus—who they knew was the promised Son of God.

How do you think they might have responded to questions about what happened that night? What questions might you have asked this innkeeper about his story of these events? How might you have responded to his explanation?

(Write your answers below.)

Prayer Time: Thank God for sending Jesus. Ask him to help you understand him better and to know him more closely.

MARIA

My little boy, Zeke (his whole name is Ezekiel), is very smart and active. Actually, he's not so little anymore. He's twelve years old now and able to take on more responsibilities around the house and for the family. He and his father, Jonas, have been working together on several projects, and Zeke seems to be accepting more and more opportunities to help his father and me. Jonas and I are very proud of him!

I have never had any occasion or reason to think that Zeke has an overactive imagination or that he would make up stories or tell a falsehood. That is why my story seems so strange and unusual. It happened three weeks ago when Jonas told me about this rabbi who has been gathering people together in the area, telling stories, praising God, and talking about how God can heal the sick and save people from their sins. All of our neighbors have been talking about him. Some of our friends have even been to one of his meetings, and they said that he is very persuasive and seems to be honest. They think he really believes what he is talking about. Of course, there are some who think he is just a rabble-rouser holding these appearances to get publicity, but Jonas was quite curious about the story. When we heard that this—Jesus, I think was his name—was going to be in our area, Jonas told me that he wanted to go and hear what all the stories were about. Of course, I agreed, and I suggested that he take Zeke with him. The meeting would be on a hillside near the sea of Tiberius, just a few miles from our home. I felt it would be good for them to go together. Zeke was old enough to join his father on trips like those, and I would have some time to catch up on some of the household chores I needed to finish. Of course, they would have to leave around midday and would be gone at the time of the evening meal, so I packed some food for them. I had just finished my week's baking the day before, so I had several barley loaves ready to eat. I packed five of those loaves into a small bag and then put two small, baked fish with them so that they wouldn't get too hungry.

The afternoon of the event came, and my men went happily on their quest. I busied myself around the house and finished other household chores as I waited to hear about their trip after they returned from their adventure. I stopped for a while to rest and tried to imagine what stories they would have to tell about their trip to hear this preacher. When they returned home later on in the early evening—it was getting dark then—Zeke came in alone. He said that his father had stopped to talk to a neighbor about what happened at the gathering to hear the rabbi. I asked him to tell me about it, but he seemed rather hesitant. That was unusual, because my son has always talked about every experience he has. He tells me about his friends and their games; he always tells me when one of them wins a game and also when they lose. When he has a positive experience at the synagogue school or when he is with his friends, he is so happy, and he always talks to me and his father about it. He also always shares with us those unhappy events that children often have. I couldn't understand why he was so reluctant to talk to me about what happened that afternoon.

When he finally decided to share his story with me, I was stunned! I know my boy doesn't lie or try to fool me. This is what he said. The rabbi had been speaking to the large crowd for some time, and they were getting restless. Some were complaining about being hungry; others were leaving to return home at mealtime. When the rabbi recognized this, he asked his friends to feed the people. Of course, there wasn't enough food to feed that many, and the men didn't know what to do. Zeke was sitting near the front of the crowd, and one of the men spotted his bag of food. He asked Zeke to share his food, and he agreed. The man—Zeke said the rabbi called him Andrew—took the food to the rabbi and told him that it was all the food he could find. The teacher took the bag, lifted it toward heaven, and started giving thanks to his God for the blessing of the food. Everybody bowed their heads when he prayed.

Zeke stopped talking for a minute. Then he looked at me and said, "Mother, you know you always told me to tell the truth about everything. I promise you that what I am going to tell you is the truth. You can ask Father when he comes home. He will tell you that I am not lying."

I hugged my son and asked him to go on with his story. He began by saying, "Mother, I don't know how all this happened. The men around the preacher started handing out food to everybody! When they finished handing out bags full of food, they went back and got some more. Mother, everybody got fed! The people said they ate barley loaves and baked fish! That's what you put in my bag! I looked around, and everybody—I mean everybody—was eating! I can't explain it! I don't understand it! Unless you were there, it would be hard for anyone to explain what happened, but I'm not lying to you. You can ask Father when he comes in."

I gave my son a big hug again and thanked him for telling me what he said he saw. I knew there had to be some reasonable explanation for what happened. Maybe there were more people with food, and they shared with the crowd. Maybe the men who were helping the preacher had brought some food with them to share with the listeners, and nobody saw where it was stored. There had to be some kind of explanation! But why did Zeke think that the people were eating the kind of food I put in his bag? I felt sure that Jonas would clear it up when he got home.

I didn't have long to wait. When my husband finally came in the back door, he had the strangest look on his face. It seemed that he didn't even see me at first. He just stared at me for several minutes. When I asked him what happened, he asked if Zeke had told me anything about what he had seen. I answered that he had told me an outrageous story, and I said I didn't quite understand why our child would make up such a story. How could anyone feed that many people with only our son's small bag of food?

Jonas then began to tell me about what happened. Amazingly, his story of what happened was exactly what Zeke had told me. He said that a man named Andrew, one of the rabbi's friends, had asked Zeke for his little bag of food. Jonas hadn't understood it, but he agreed and told Zeke to give it to him. After all the people had been fed—he said it sounded strange, but it was true!—there were at least twelve baskets of food left over! Jonas seemed to be overwhelmed by what he had seen and experienced. Now, my husband is a very practical man and is not easily convinced about new and unusual events, but this time, his serious explanation and retelling of the situation seemed to affect him in a way I had not seen in a long time. He was obviously deeply moved by what he saw and experienced at that gathering on the hillside. He said that he wanted to find out more about this rabbi-teacher and see if there were any other unusual events that people had heard about.

The next day, Jonas took Zeke with him to try to find out where this teacher would be traveling next. He is determined to find out more about this miracle worker. I know my husband very well, and if this man is teaching anywhere near, Jonas will find him. I'll be anxious to hear the results of his search. Maybe he'll take me with him next time!

THINK ABOUT IT!

1. Consider the Word

Read John 6:1–14; Matthew 14:15–21; Mark 6:32–44; Luke 9:12–17.

2. Consider Your Response

Think of a time when you were in a large crowd—maybe a family gathering, a school or church function, a sports event, or a similar situation—and there was no provision for the crowd to eat. How did you feel? What opportunities were there for satisfying the hunger of those present?

Now, think of a time when someone perhaps offered to treat you to a full meal when you were hungry. How did you feel toward that person? Imagine being in that crowd when Jesus served dinner! What an amazing event that must have been! Can you imagine how you might have responded?

(Write your response below.)

Prayer Time: Thank God for his care and daily provisions for you. Ask him to bless those who are less fortunate.

EZRA

I know I should have postponed that business trip, but my boat needed repairs, and the only place I could find what I needed was fifty miles away. I had to leave two days early in order to arrive before the Sabbath day, when all business stops. My wife wasn't feeling well when I left. She had a high fever and needed special attention, and I hated to leave her, but without my boat, I can't make a living. I had to get it fixed. Besides, my daughter lives close by, and she and her husband assured me that they would take good care of my wife.

Now, my daughter is a very caring person. She married a hardworking fisherman named Peter, and they seemed very happy for a while, but lately he's been gone a lot. He's been away from his boat for several days at a time, following this rabbi who seems to have caught his attention for some strange reason. I can't figure out what he sees in this man. He just goes around from village to village, teaching in the synagogues, in the street, and on the mountainsides, anywhere he can gather a crowd. Peter says he talks about God as heavenly Father and how we should all just love one another. Now, we've all been brought up to believe that one day our Messiah will come, and I heard that many people think this rabbi is the Promised One, the Messiah who will redeem Israel and pull us out from under the yoke of Roman rule. After all, the Roman authorities have made it tough on us, and we could use someone to bail us out of our difficulties. They've imposed so many taxes on us that it's hard to make a decent living anymore. Peter's father, Jonah, has tried to deal with his son's absence, but the boy seems pretty determined to follow this man. Jonah told me that Andrew, Peter's brother, talked him into meeting this rabbi, and one day they just walked away from their fishing business. My friend Zebedee also said that his sons, James and John, left their jobs at the fishing boat to follow this man. Oh, they all check back once in a while to see how things are going with their families, but this teacher seems to have some kind of strange hold on all these young men.

But let me get on with my story. When I returned from my trip to get my boat fixed, I learned that my wife's condition had gotten progressively worse while I was gone, and she was unable to get out of bed. She couldn't even talk to our sons and tell them what was wrong. Her fever was so high that their hands were hot when they touched her. Everyone around was afraid that she was going to die. Neighbors were in and out of the house, bringing food and offering remedies, but nothing seemed to help. She just kept getting sicker and sicker.

Finally, Peter, who had come home earlier when he heard that she was sick, decided to take over the situation. He's always been thoughtful of us and good to our daughter, so this was typical of him. Oh, he can be hotheaded and stubborn at times, even impulsive in some situations, but when push comes to shove, you can depend on him to do the right thing. He sent a message to that teacher friend of his who was speaking in the local synagogue and told him that his mother-in-law was sick. He begged him to come and see what he could do. Peter told us later that he had seen this man do unusual and almost miraculous things with sick people, and Peter trusted that he could do the same thing for my wife.

Jesus—that was the rabbi's name—came to our house later that same afternoon. Peter said that there was a crowd of people around, but they stood back out of the way when Jesus entered. The rabbi asked Peter how my wife was feeling, and Peter told him that she was very sick; she couldn't talk and was running a high fever, and everyone was very worried that she might not get well. Jesus asked all the people to go outside. Peter and our daughter were the only ones in the room. As Jesus stood near the bed, he spoke gently to my wife, took her by the hand, and told her to stand up. Peter later told us that she opened her eyes, looked up at Jesus, smiled, and said, "Thank you, sir." She stood up slowly, took a deep breath, then went to the door and told the neighbors who were gathered there that she was feeling better. She thanked them for their concern and told them that she would call on them again if she needed them. Then—and this is just like her—she went into the kitchen and started preparing dinner! She showed no signs of a fever; she was speaking clearly and distinctly and shooing everyone out of the kitchen so that she could feed her family!

When I finally returned a few days after the incident and our daughter told me the whole story, it was hard for me to believe. My wife is a very strong woman. She has always worked hard caring for our home, and she had always been able to manage the children as they were growing up. She insisted that our sons get experience in the fishing business early so that they would have a career when we were no longer able to provide for them. It wasn't a surprise when our daughter met this fisherman Peter and married him. My wife has always been friendly and kind to our neighbors and wanted to help them if they ever needed anything. I can't remember her ever being sick enough to take to her bed. Yet, I know my daughter doesn't lie, and I have no reason to doubt Peter. While I don't always agree with him, I know he is sincere and loves and respects us. I can't believe that he would make up a story like this, and after I spoke to some of the neighbors, they all confirmed the presence of the rabbi and the unusually quick response of my wife.

When I later discussed the situation with my wife, she had trouble explaining what happened. She said that she had suddenly gotten weaker, she felt hot and then cold, her head was hurting badly, and she couldn't concentrate on what she was doing. Our daughter insisted that she go to bed, but she didn't want to do that because there was too much to do. But when Peter came home, she decided that she would let them arrange for her care. She has always thought highly of our son-in-law and believes that his decisions are wise. When he decided to call his rabbi friend, she told him to go ahead. She doesn't remember much after that discussion, but she does remember feeling a strong hand on her arm and a gentle voice speaking to her. She thought it was Peter at first, but the voice was gentler, yet firm enough to get her attention. The voice spoke to her and told her to get up from her bed. She said that she looked up at him and saw the kindest eyes she had ever seen. She said that there was something unusual about his eyes. They seemed to be looking right into her soul, as she explained it. Then the man gently took her hand, helped her out of bed, smiled at her and then at Peter and my daughter, then left the house. My wife felt a strong pulsation in her body, her strength immediately returned to her, and she was ready to resume her duties around the house. She said that she couldn't really understand or explain what had happened, but she knew that the man who came to the house with Peter that day was somebody special. He didn't appear to be a doctor, but he was able to make her sickness go away with only a touch. She remembered that his hand was very warm, yet strong, and it seemed to have a strange tingle of some sort, something she had never felt before.

Now, it's not that I doubt what occurred in our home. There are just too many people who will swear to the truth of what happened that Sabbath day, and my wife has never been one to tell stories that aren't true. I just want to know where this Jesus gets his awesome power—the power to heal sick people and give them new strength. Peter, I know, can tell me more about him. I think he and I will have to have a long talk about this—that is, if I can catch him for a few minutes on his next trip home! Maybe he'll even introduce me to this teacher one day. I think I'll ask him to do that the next time he comes home! I'd like to hear that young man's personal account of what happened that day in my home. Could this visitor to our home really be the one we've heard so many people talk about—the Promised One? The Messiah? The Savior? I'd like to know for myself, and I'd like to personally thank him for what he did for my wife. It's something to look forward to. Maybe soon!

Think about It!

1. Consider the Word

Read Luke 4:38; Matthew 8:14–15; Mark 1:29–31.

2. Consider Your Response

Have you ever been away from home and worried about what would happen while you were gone? What if a child got hurt? What if a family member had a serious accident? What if a burglar tried to break into your house? Is there someone you could call who could check what was happening?

What if you were alone and got very sick? Is there someone you could call for help? Think of how you would respond in each of these situations. What would you tell those people, or what would you ask them to do for you?

(Write your answers below.)

Prayer Time: Thank God for your family and/or the friends on whom you can depend. Thank him for always being ready to help you. He will never leave you or forsake you!

OLIVIA

My best friend, Anna, has had quite a remarkable transformation in her life, and if anyone needed to change, she would be the best example. It's quite a story, but it really is true. I've known her since we were children, and she has always seemed to need attention. In her teen years, she always tried to get attention from the boys. She was first called a big flirt, but later everyone quietly referred to her as a tramp.

I didn't like that. I never called her names, even when she started offering her body to any man who paid special attention to her. I even tried to talk to her to try to find out why she did all the things everybody talked about. Her only answer was, "Why not? Nobody gets hurt. Besides, I enjoy it! You ought to try it sometime!"

Of course, I never participated in that kind of activity. My parents always told me that I must save myself for my husband, whom they would select for me.

Well, as we grew into young womanhood, I got married and started our family. Anna and I lost touch with each other. I did hear that she had moved away from home, but nobody seemed to know or care where she was. Rumors were that she was selling herself to any man who would offer her money. I was so sorry to hear those things. We used to be such good friends, and I could never understand why she chose that sinful way of life.

Now, here is where the story takes an unusual turn. I learned from some neighbors that Anna had come back to town. Her father had died, and her aging mother needed someone to care for her. Somehow Anna had heard about the situation, and, to her credit, she decided to return home to care for her mother. Even though her mother knew the kind of life Anna had been living, she still loved her daughter and had never given up hope that somehow and someday she would change her lifestyle and come home.

Well, when I learned that Anna had finally returned, I decided to take some food to their home and see how my friend was doing. We had a wonderful reunion! I couldn't believe how good she looked! I had heard rumors about her way of life from many people, and I thought that she would look disheveled or weak or sick, unhappy or guilty, but that wasn't the case. When we met, she ran to me, hugged me tightly, and said, "Oh, Olivia! I've got so much to tell you!" She looked remarkably healthy, strong, confident, and, yes, as beautiful as I remembered her. It was just like old times again, just two good friends rejoicing over a long-delayed and unexpected reunion.

After a few minutes of joyous remembering, Anna began her story. It seems that she had been with a married man in the park behind the temple when they were caught by some of the temple officials. She was taken into their custody, and they dragged her into the city square to be stoned, the usual religious punishment for adultery. Suddenly this man—she said he was a rabbi or something—stepped into the scene, stood in the middle of the crowd, and turned around slowly, looking deeply into the eyes of each of the men who were holding her. After he carefully scanned the faces of each of the men, he then stooped over and started moving his finger along the ground, obviously writing something. Then he stood up, looked around again, and told them to turn her loose, stop their threats against her, and leave her alone. Then, Anna said, this man turned to the crowd and spoke in a very firm and authoritative voice. "If any of you is without sin, you may throw the first stone."

"There was a hush that fell over the crowd," Anna said. She continued. The men all began slowly to move away from her, and some of them seemed to be hanging their heads in shame. One by one, they began to throw their stones on the ground. Some of them were mumbling, maybe even cursing, but they left her alone.

Then she said the rabbi took her hand and lifted her up from the ground where she had been pushed. She said she had never seen anyone like him. His eyes were soft, gentle, and forgiving; his hands were strong and warm; his voice was tender, yet forceful. Then, she said, the rabbi spoke directly to her. She again remarked about the tenderness in his voice when he said, "Your sins are forgiven; now go and sin no more." When he spoke those words to her, she said she had a strong sensation of importance, of being somehow special, of being loved, actually loved for herself and not just for her body. I asked her if she ever found out who he was. She said someone told her that they heard his name was Jesus.

Anna's face glowed as she recalled the encounter with this rabbi, this Jesus. She explained that she had been ashamed to come back home and had been living with and caring for an elderly widow in a small town not far from our town. "Oh, Olivia!" she exclaimed. "You can't believe how much the burden and the shame of my life and my body has been taken away! This rabbi, this teacher, this great man looked at me in a way I had never seen before, not with lust, not desire, not contempt, not pity, but with the look of a loving father and dear friend who cared for my soul, not just wanting my body. For the first time in my life, I felt special. I felt loved. I actually felt respected! I never knew that feeling before. That man, that kind teacher, actually seemed to be in touch with the God I heard about as a child. I can't remember feeling like this since I was a little girl. Can you understand what has happened to me?"

It took me a while to process her story. Anna and I had gone our separate ways, but now in these special moments, I felt our friendship—almost like sisters—had become real again. She was so sincere and honest in her story. She looked so much like the friend I had known years ago. There seemed to be a special kind of tie that bound us together again. Maybe we can go together to hear this rabbi speak when we find him. I'd really like to know more about him. There's something rare, indeed remarkable, maybe even godly about a preacher who can cause such a change in my childhood friend. Maybe I can understand Anna's story even more if I can hear and see this special person, this teacher, this rabbi who caused such a miraculous change in my friend. I hope to be able to find him and hear more of what he has to say. I know it will be an unforgettable experience!

THINK ABOUT IT!

1. Consider the Word

Read John 8:1–11.

2. Consider Your Response

What are some of the names that you have heard applied to women like Anna? Have you ever called someone by any of these names? Why do you think women would get involved in that kind of lifestyle?

If someone in your family lived this kind of life, how would you feel when you were around her? What would be the Christian's treatment of someone who lived this way? What could you do to help someone in this situation? Or could you? Why or why not?

(Write your responses below.)

Prayer Time: Thank God for his forgiving power to change lives. Ask him to help you understand situations that might force someone into that kind of lifestyle and to grant compassion in such a situation.

JACOB

I have worked as a roofer for many years, and I have encountered strange people and unusual events through these years, but just a few months ago, I heard of something that is really hard to believe. A friend of mine, Amos, asked me to repair his roof, which I had built for him just a few years ago. It seems that somehow a group of men climbed onto the roof, tore it up so that there was a large hole exposed, and let someone down onto the floor. When I asked him about how it happened, he told a strange story.

There had been rumors that a popular rabbi was going from town to town with a group of his friends, preaching about God and how to get closer to him, and some even said that he could heal people with serious diseases and people with all kinds of physical problems. I had heard rumors about this rabbi, and Amos had asked him to come to his home for a meal and to lead his neighbors in a time of worship and teaching. This group of followers—the rabbi called them his disciples—go with him and make arrangements for him to meet people and preach to them. Amos's home is large enough to accommodate a large group, and he willingly offered his hospitality to this rabbi and his friends.

It seems that when this group came into town, a local man named Eli, who usually has to be carried wherever he goes because he is paralyzed with something called palsy, had some friends who wanted to bring him to the rabbi, whose name was—I think they called him Jesus. They hoped this miracle worker could heal their friend from his paralysis. However, by the time Eli's friends got to his house, picked him up and carried him to Amos's home, where this Jesus was speaking, the house was already full of onlookers, and there was no room for the man to get to this healer.

Amos then said he later learned that one of the men—he didn't say which one—had the idea of crawling up on top of the house, tearing open a hole in the roof, and letting their friend down through the opening in front of the healer. It seemed like a bad idea to tear up a roof, but this man said it would be worth it if this Jesus could heal their friend. After a long discussion among the men, they agreed to do it. It must have taken quite a while to accomplish the work, but nobody seemed to pay much attention to what was taking place, and the noise it made didn't seem to bother those who were listening to the teachings of this man Jesus. Amos said that he was so engrossed in the rabbi's message that he didn't pay any attention to the noise.

Now comes the strange part. After a short break in the rabbi's teaching, Amos got up to stretch his muscles—cramped from sitting on the floor. When he stood up, he was amazed when he raised his head to see his roof opened up and this paralyzed man being eased down through the ceiling on a large mat held up by ropes on each corner. When he finally reached the floor of the room, Eli was directly in front of the healer. Of course, the whole crowd was amazed, and the situation seemed on the brink of chaos. There was lots of gasping and yelling among the members of the crowd, but Amos finally got them quiet and said for the people to listen to what Jesus had to say.

Now—and here's where the story takes another strange turn—this man, Jesus, didn't seem to be surprised at what was happening. He quieted the crowd and then took the paralyzed man by the hand and said, "Your sins are forgiven." Well, this brought another noisy response from the crowd, especially among leaders of the local synagogue who had come to see what Jesus was up to. Then Jesus turned toward the other rabbis and asked them if it was easier to say their sins were forgiven or to tell the crippled man to get up and walk. Now—you probably won't believe this; I didn't at first—Jesus told that poor man to pick up his bed and walk! And you know what? That's what he did! Amos said that he just moved his body slowly along the floor, raised himself up on his knees, then got his feet steadily together, pushed himself up off the ground, raised his hands in the air, picked up that mat, and walked away! I honestly couldn't believe what my friend told me, but Amos swears that the story is true, and he's always been honest with me. He said that the crowd was stunned! Nobody spoke for a few moments. Then they all started cheering and praising God. As you might expect, the Pharisees, who I understand were continually trying to find something against Jesus, started calling this miracle a hoax and claimed that Eli wasn't really crippled, that he had been faking his disability for years just to get out of work. Yet the people in the room knew the whole story and paid no attention to those objections. They just kept on cheering and praising God!

Of course, I've had a hard time understanding what Amos told me, but I know it has to be true, not only because Amos is an honest man but because I saw Eli—the crippled man—last week as he was walking down the road toward town. I walked over to him just to be sure it was the same man I had seen for years begging for food and help while lying crippled on his mat in town. He was pleasant, smiling a lot, and anxious to tell his story. I really wanted to know all about what had happened to him, and he spoke freely, smiling and gesturing while he explained his feelings and what he was doing now. He said that he had endured pain for many years and had been overlooked by most of the community because he had to beg for a living. Sometimes he had been hungry because nobody would give him food, and he couldn't work because of his paralysis. He had prayed for many years that he would somehow find someone who could help him regain his strength and be able to walk again. When he heard about this man, Jesus, and how he had been healing people in other towns, he hoped that somehow he would be able to meet him and find a way to get close enough to ask this rabbi for healing. However, his paralysis was so strong that he couldn't travel for any long trips and couldn't move well enough to get closer when Jesus finally came to his town. Fortunately, his friends dared to make the move to the rooftop and got him to Jesus.

Eli teared up when he finished telling me his story. He said that when Jesus spoke to him, his whole body shivered as if someone had poured cold water all over him. He trembled, shook, cried out loud, and screamed, "Praise God!" Well, that caused another uproar, he said, and the whole meeting was turned into a praise session—except for those local Pharisees. They scoffed at this "magic" that had happened and said it was all a hoax. When they stormed angrily out of the house, the whole room exploded into praise and thanksgiving for what they had heard and seen. Eli said he then just picked up his mat, walked to his house, and thanked God for the miracle of which he had been a part.

The story that Amos told and the story that Eli shared are both exactly alike, so I have no reason to doubt either of them. I do know that when Amos asked me to repair his roof, he seemed to be a changed man. He was quieter and more thoughtful. He agreed with me on both materials and prices for repairing his roof, and he agreed that we both had shared a remarkable experience—he as a witness and I as a believer, because we have both been eyewitnesses.

I'm going to be telling this story wherever and whenever I am called to build or repair any roof in the future. I think I ought to do this because it has really changed my outlook on life. I hope I will someday run into this healer so that I can tell him what Amos's story and Eli's healing have meant to me. My life is forever changed because of this experience, and I don't think I'll ever be the same again. You just don't see miracles every day!

THINK ABOUT IT!

1. Consider the Word

Read Mark 2:1–12; Luke 5:17–26.

2. Consider Your Response

Have you ever been beside someone who was quite ill, and the physician brought news that healing was taking place? Have you ever been very sick and wondered if you would recover? Have you heard stories of others who may have experienced a situation like this? If not, try to imagine yourself in a room where this situation became a reality. How do you think you might respond? Would you share your story with others? Would you shout praises to God? What would you do if you wanted to share your response? How would you share it? Do you think the experience would have any lasting effect in your life? Why or why not?

(Write your responses below.)

Prayer Time: Thank God for his healing power. Ask him to give you a sense of compassion for those who may have physical disabilities or illnesses.

IBRAM

My brother Timaeus had lots of difficulty in his life, but he always had great courage and remarkable strength to deal with what life had for him to experience. The greatest sorrow in his life, however, was when the doctors told him that his little son, Bartimaeus, his pride and joy, was blind. Both Timaeus and his wife were heartbroken. They had looked forward to the birth of their baby and were overjoyed when they realized that they had a beautiful baby boy. The news that he was born blind devastated them, but their faith carried them through. They took very good care of him through the years, but after they died, Bartimaeus, grown to adulthood, had to find some way to take care of himself. There isn't much that a blind man can do, so he eventually wound up on the streets, begging for food or for any help that passersby would throw his way.

For several years, he had stationed himself in a special place at the edge of Jericho so that whoever was entering or leaving the town would have to pass by him. He was well-known to the citizens and seemed to catch the attention of many of the people who wandered into the city. He would call out to them, and most would toss him some food or occasionally a piece of clothing that they didn't want anymore. He would eventually find someone who would help him back into his little house, where he would settle in for the night. My wife and I would check on him occasionally just to be sure that he was all right, and often, my wife would bring him a special meal that she had prepared.

One day, we heard that this popular rabbi called Jesus was coming toward our town. Stories were circulating that he was able to perform miracles like healing and also that he could explain serious teachings about God so that even children could understand. People said he had a special way with children and the sick. We thought about this and decided that we would go into town when he came and see if all the stories were true.

We walked into the city and started looking for Bartimaeus. He wasn't in his usual resting place beside the road. We looked all over town and couldn't find him. Of course, we became very concerned and started asking some of the people who were still gathered at the entrance to the city. Most of the people seemed to be still talking about this rabbi and all the things he had done. One of the people—I think his name was Demas—said that Bartimaeus had received his sight and had walked away following this Jesus. Bartimaeus was no longer blind? He had been born blind and had never been able to move about much on his own. This was unbelievable news, and my wife and I decided to try to find someone who could explain exactly what had happened.

We finally met a friend, Damon, whom we had known for a long time and who knew Bartimaeus's story. This man told us the most remarkable story, and we couldn't question him because he had seen the event with his own eyes. He told us that our nephew had been in his usual place when the rabbi was on his way out of the city. He said that Bartimaeus heard the people talking as Jesus was passing him, and he started crying out to him. He was yelling something like, "Son of David, have mercy on me!" People were trying to calm him down, but he kept calling out to this Jesus to have mercy on him. Damon said that Jesus stopped, looked at him, and asked someone to bring this man to him. One of the men called out to Bartimaeus and told him that Jesus wanted to talk to him. Bartimaeus threw off his cloak and, hearing Jesus's voice, made his way slowly toward the rabbi. When Jesus asked him what he wanted, Bartimaeus replied, "I want to see." And then—and I believe Damon—Jesus told him that his faith had made him able to see. Then, as the crowd watched, Bartimaeus rubbed his eyes, held his head up toward the heavens, and cried out to God, "Praise God! I can see! I can see! I can see!"

The crowd was suddenly quiet, Damon said. They just couldn't believe what they had seen happen right before their eyes. Many of them had known Bartimaeus from the time he was a child. They knew that he had been born blind. They had watched him grow up and had seen him by the entrance gate every day. There was no question that he was really blind. There was no question that he had been begging for food for years at the entrance gate. Many of the people had given him food throughout the years and felt sorry for him because he had to beg for a living. Now, most of them stood stunned as they saw the former blind man shouting praise to God for his sudden ability to see his surroundings and the people who had helped him survive throughout the years.

Damon had no reason to make up such a story, and Bartimaeus was nowhere to be found. We wanted to find him and hear his side of the story, but we didn't see him anywhere. When we began to talk to some of the others standing around the area, we learned that he had followed Jesus and his helpers as they left the city and headed down the road to Jerusalem. He had been in such a hurry that he left his cloak lying in the street, right where he had spent so many years begging for food.

We heard sometime later that this Jesus was tried and convicted by the Pharisees, and they sentenced Jesus to death by crucifixion like some common criminal. We wondered if Bartimaeus was present when all of that happened and where he is now. We haven't heard from him, and nobody in town has heard anything from him. He must have joined those men who followed Jesus everywhere and are now traveling around the country speaking to people about their rabbi—the one who performed so many miracles and who convinced hearers that he was indeed the Son of God who had been prophesied through the years. My wife and I have had some serious discussions about this possibility. I really don't see how we could doubt it. After all, there was a real miracle in our family. Our nephew, our blind nephew, received his sight from this man. There could be no doubt about that! There were too many witnesses to the incident. People still talk about it today. There are groups around the city who gather regularly to celebrate the work of this man, Jesus. I think my wife and I will try to find one of those groups, hear more of these stories about this miracle worker, and join their discussions about this Jesus. Maybe he really was the Son of God! If that's true, wouldn't that be a great discovery?

Think about It!

1. Consider the Word

Read Mark 10:46–52; Matthew 20:29–34; Luke 18:35–43.

2. Consider Your Response

Have you ever been associated with anyone who was blind? How did you respond or react to that person? Did you question the cause of the blindness? Did you ask how they were able to manage their everyday activities? If you haven't been around a blind person, cover your eyes with both hands and try to make your way around your house or apartment. Can you begin to understand how a person without sight must feel?

Would you offer to help someone who is blind if you came in contact with that person? What do you think you would feel? Pity? Compassion? Understanding? Sadness? Confusion? Helplessness? What could you offer to do for that person? What could you do to make that person more comfortable with you?

(Write your responses below.)

Prayer Time: Thank God for his healing power and his compassion for those in need. Ask him to give you a greater understanding and compassion for anyone with a physical disability.

SARAI

My younger sister Hannah has had a difficult life in her later years. Although she was always a pretty girl, she was so shy that she never developed close friends or any male companions. She was pleasant enough around family but was never comfortable around people she didn't know well. She liked to prepare food for neighbors who were in need and was always generous with what limited funds she had inherited from our parents. When she became old enough, she decided to move out on her own. Our parents tried to discourage her from trying to live by herself, but she was determined to try. She moved into a small house at the edge of town, and for several years she seemed to be doing quite well.

A few years after she moved away from home, we began to notice a change in her. She seemed to be bowing down to everyone she met and didn't straighten up like she used to do. We didn't think too much about it for a while, but as the years went by, she seemed to be bending over much more, and soon she was so stooped over that she couldn't even raise her body to look anyone in the eye. Her innate shyness kept her from discussing her condition with anyone, even though we tried to get her to talk about her feelings. She would just turn her body away from us and get very quiet. After a few years, we stopped trying to understand her, and she grew further and further away from her family, not coming home for visits and acting reluctant to see us when we went to check on her. Friends told us she was very faithful about attending worship services at the synagogue. According to those who also attended regularly, her presence rather inspired the worshippers. According to their information, she would be at the synagogue early on the Sabbath day and find a place where she could sit down. Her back was crippled badly by this time—it's been more than fifteen years now that she has wrestled with this bent body—and she was heard to ask often, "How blue is the sky today?" This became her regular question, and we were told that the people around her would smile as they gave her the answer. The priests at the synagogue were kind to her, we were told, and they often publicly acknowledged her faithfulness to the worship services.

At a recent Sabbath gathering at the synagogue, the priests had allowed a popular rabbi to teach, and a large crowd had gathered to hear him. His reputation had spread among the people, and a large part of the city had gathered to hear him. It was rumored that he had been traveling around the country with a group of followers and had been able to heal sick people. It was also said that he taught special lessons about God's love, and he seemed to have some sort of special connection to God and the old prophets who had promised a chosen one to be sent from God. Everyone who heard him seemed almost spellbound by his message.

It was reported that the rabbi—I think she said later that his name was Jesus—stopped in the middle of his message, looked at Hannah sitting quietly at the side of the crowd, and told her to come to the front where he was teaching. Friends said that she struggled to raise herself and had great difficulty standing up. She was bent so far over that she could not even see the faces of the two neighbors who took her arms and helped her walk toward the rabbi. She said, "Thank you," quietly to those who helped her and moved slowly toward the teacher. People who were worshipping that day were startled when the speaker told her that she was immediately healed from her painful, crippled back. I understand that there was a great gasp through the crowd when she raised her head, looked around, and then slowly began to straighten her back—that back that had bent her almost double for all those years. She seemed without pain but had a surprising, even startled, look on her face. They said that she gradually rose to her full height, looked slowly around at everybody who was staring at her, and began to sing and shout praises to God. This was so unlike my shy sister that the people in the crowd just held their breath while she sang praises. I was told that the synagogue leader was stunned and started complaining that the rabbi had desecrated the Sabbath by healing, an act that called for work on his part, and no labor is permitted on that holy day. The synagogue has always been a quiet, worshipful place, and those who attend regularly had never seen anything like this before. People also said that this Jesus responded by asking them about saving an animal in distress on the Sabbath. This seemed to quiet the ruler, and the crowd began to shout and praise God for Hannah's healing, unusual activity for Sabbath worshippers.

When I heard all these stories about what had happened to Hannah, I sent word to her that I wanted to hear her side of the story. A few days later, I heard a knock at my door. When I opened it, there she stood, straight and tall, beautiful, smiling, and talking about what a beautiful blue sky she was enjoying. This was a different sister from the one I had known and loved all those years while she suffered with that crippled back. She was no longer the shy, embarrassed crippled sister but a vibrant, lovely woman, matured now but still my baby sister. We hugged each other tightly, and when we finally settled down to talk, I asked her to tell me if what I had heard about her encounter with the rabbi was true.

When she began to talk, there was a different look on her face. I would describe it as *radiance*. She seemed to glow. Her smile was not forced now; it was genuine joy that she was feeling. While I watched her tell her side of the story, I realized that I truly was witnessing the result of a miracle. Her recollection of the event at the synagogue was exactly as I had heard it from those who were present. She said that this Jesus called her to come to where he was sitting. He didn't ask her any questions; he didn't preach to her; he didn't even touch her. He only spoke the healing words that I had heard from others. She said that at that moment she began to feel a strange tingling in her body. Her back shivered a little, as if someone had poured water over her. Then she felt a strange kind of pulling in her shoulders. She had to move around to try to shake it off, but as she moved, she began to straighten up and began to be able to see faces in the crowd. She turned to look in the face of the rabbi. She said he was smiling gently at her, as if he was pleased with her response. When she turned back to look at the people, she saw the synagogue rulers looking angrily at the rabbi. She remarked about what a difference she saw in the angry face of the priest and the gentle, compassionate smile of the rabbi.

When she rose to leave, I asked her to stay for a while and visit. I wanted to hear more about this teacher and his message. I wanted to know where his power to heal came from. I wanted to know where he was now and how I could find a way to hear him in person. She said that she had heard that he was on his way to Jerusalem. No one seemed to know much more about him. She said she had been asked to share her story with some of those who accepted him as the chosen one of God. They wanted her to explain how she felt now as compared to when she was crippled. She said that she wasn't sure she could put into words what a difference her healing had made in her attitude toward others, especially those who had called her a cripple and had ignored her discomfort. She said that her forgiveness should accompany thanksgiving for those who had always been kind to her. As she said, "I've got a lot to think about, Sarai. Please ask God to help me do what I need to do to share my story with others."

Because of Hannah's story and her miraculous healing, I think I'm going to try to find out more about this miracle worker. What he did for my sister is probably just an example of many other things that he can do and has done for others. I hope he comes through our town on his way back from Jerusalem. Maybe after he finishes his mission there, he'll come back this way. I hope so. I'd like to thank him personally for giving me back my baby sister—now so perfectly straight and tall. What a special gift he gave our family!

Think about It!

1. Consider the Word

Read Luke 13:10–17.

2. Consider Your Response

Have you ever been around anyone who could be considered crippled? Today, we speak of the *handicapped* or *physically disabled* or other appropriate terms. How do you feel in the presence of people in that situation? Do you feel sorry for them? Do you want to help them? Do you offer to accompany them or drive them to their appointments? Do you ask questions about their condition? Be honest now. Do you try to avoid contact with them? Why or why not? What if a member of your family was involved in an accident of some kind that left them handicapped? Would your attitude be changed, or would your inherent concern for them take over? Explain how you think you would feel.

(Write your responses below.)

Prayer Time: Thank God for his great compassion for those who have special physical needs. Ask him to help you have more understanding of what people with those kinds of disabilities face each day.

PAULUS

My cousin Zacchaeus—we call him Zach—is rather eccentric; at least, that's the word I use to describe him. Other people refer to him as an oddball, conceited, selfish, and, of course, "Shorty." He's the shortest member of our entire family and has always had to have help reaching things that were too high for him. And another thing about him. Of all the jobs he could have had—I think people felt sorry for him—he decided to become a tax collector!

When we first heard about his new job, we couldn't believe it! Hadn't he gotten enough ridicule and unkind remarks about his height and his unpredictable behavior? But he seemed to be quite successful in his position, and after a while, he became quite wealthy. I hope he's being honest in his work, but, as you know, tax collectors in our city almost always have unkind reputations about their work. Most people think they become rich by cheating, but nobody can do anything about it. They are powerful people, and nobody seems to want to challenge their honesty because of the repercussions they could experience when tax time approaches.

Anyway, my story about my cousin has some rather interesting highlights. Zach has never been someone who would sit around and have a friendly conversation with his family. He has no real friends to socialize with, so my wife and I invite him for dinner occasionally just to let him know that he is still a part of our family. He has sort of an inferiority complex about his height, so we try not to mention anything or do anything that would make him feel more self-conscious.

Well, we invited him over last week to help celebrate my birthday. What a surprise we had! When he came in the door, he was carrying several bags. We couldn't imagine what was in those bags. He had been to our birthday celebrations on several occasions but had never brought any gifts or acknowledgments of the celebration. Also, when he came in, he was smiling! I don't think I had ever seen him smile before. He'd always been very quiet on those occasions. Oh, once in a while, he would speak up and tell a story of some experience with a reluctant taxpayer. Occasionally, he would get a little animated about an encounter he had with someone who had made fun of his height or had spoken angrily to him about his profession. However, most of the time when he visited, he was congenial but subdued.

At my birthday gathering, as I was saying, he began to open the bags he was carrying. He gave me a fine pair of sandals. For my wife, he had a very nice pottery collection for her kitchen, and for our two boys, a pair of sandals for each, saying he hoped they would fit. They did. He explained that he had missed some birthday celebrations in the past and wanted to "catch up on things," as he said.

When we finally sat down to talk and thank him, he began to tell a story that was hard to believe. He told us that his whole attitude toward life had changed. He had been caught up in a crowd that had gathered to see and hear a traveling rabbi who had arrived in Jericho. Rumors around the city were that he had somehow been able to cure the eyesight of a blind man. It was Bartimaeus! Now, Bartimaeus was well-known because he always sat beside the road begging for help. Most everybody in the city of Jericho knew him and had often given him meals. If he really had been healed, Zach wanted to hear more about this miracle worker.

Now, here's the way he told the rest of the story. I'll try to remember his exact words. "When I got into town, the crowd had already gathered, and I couldn't see or hear anything. I decided to climb up on the limb of that beautiful sycamore tree near the center of town, close to the area where the man would have to pass. I didn't mean to cause any trouble, but this man moved toward the tree and stopped. Then—and this stunned me—he turned around, looked up into the tree directly at me and—you probably won't believe this—he called me by my name! His voice was strong and very authoritative. When he told me to come down out of the tree, I thought he was angry, but he announced that he wanted to come to my house! Well, this didn't make the people in the crowd very happy, and they started complaining about this popular healer going home with a sinner, as they all called me.

"We had a remarkable evening," Zach continued. "He explained God's plan for his people to help each other and that all people really belonged to God. He stressed the *all* part of his message. Before the evening was over, I knew my life was going to be different. I was changed by this man's message and the fact that he singled me out for the evening's visit. I'm a different person because of this Jesus—that was his name. Now, here's what I'm going to do."

Zach then explained his plans. He was going to turn over half of his income to feed the poor. He was going to repay the people he had cheated through the years—yes, he admitted his dishonesty. He was going to repay them four times over what he had taken from them. When he told us this, it was hard to believe, but he seemed sincere. I really believe now that he has had a great change in his life. People in town report that he has been visiting them and giving them money that he said he owed them. It really is a miracle that we have witnessed in Zach's life. I guess this rabbi—this Jesus—must be a real miracle worker if he could bring about this remarkable change in my cousin. I hope I'll be able to hear him myself someday. Maybe I'll try to find out where he will be going next and make a trip to hear him. Maybe there are more miracles that he will do. I'd like to be present to see another one. Maybe soon!

Think about It!

1. Consider the Word

Read Luke 19:1–11.

2. Consider Your Response

Have you ever wondered how very short people manage to deal with their height? Think about how a tiny housewife might deal with cabinet contents. How might a carpenter handle working around windows or large doors? How might a gardener or landscaper trim tall bushes? What about a teacher reaching for books on a high library shelf?

Small children sometimes are harassed by larger classmates. What can an adult (parent, teacher, etc.) do to handle the situation?

Imagine yourself as shorter than five feet tall. What kind of problems might you encounter? How do you think you would react to people who constantly remarked about your height?

(Write your responses below.)

Prayer Time: Thank God for your health, your physical strength, and your ability to lead a normal life. If you have a physical disability, ask him to help you deal with it in a strong and gracious manner.

ESTHER

My brother has always been a little strange. Even when he was just a little boy, he was hard to handle. He would say words that had no meaning, talk when there was nobody around, throw temper tantrums with no provocation, and run away for hours. We had to constantly watch him to keep him from hurting himself or falling into danger. One time, my father and I had to pull him out of a well where he had fallen. He almost drowned that time. Another time, I found him out in the woods just staring at the trees. His arms were bleeding badly, and I realized he had been cutting himself with the bloody rocks lying there on the ground. He couldn't—or wouldn't—sleep, so our family had to take turns staying awake to keep him from leaving in the middle of the night to go who knows where.

My father and mother tried everything they knew to get him help, but the doctors couldn't figure out what was wrong and just chalked it up to demon possession. All of our neighbors were scared to be around him, and they wouldn't even come to our house when we invited them for a meal. In his teens, he was a holy terror! We were all beginning to be afraid of what he might do when he started one of his rages. Most of the time, we didn't even know what set him off. He would scream, throw things, curse, and stomp around the house, lashing out at anyone who happened to be in his way. Our only recourse at those times was just to stay out of his way. Of course, all his life, we had prayed that God would somehow cure him of his demons. We even called in the priests from our synagogue to pray for him, but we couldn't get him to stay in their presence long enough to do any good. They finally just ignored our pleas for help, so we gave up on that angle.

When he was in his early twenties, my brother left home one night when my father had fallen asleep on his night watch. We looked for him everywhere—in the village, in the woods, out on the road to town, down by the lake—but no one had seen him or heard anything about him. We even went into some of the neighboring villages to ask about him. No luck there either. Even though he had been such a troubled soul and had caused the family so much anguish, we still loved him. After all, he was still part of our family, and we at least wanted to know that he was safe. We finally gave up looking for him.

He had been gone for several years when a strange thing happened. While we were together eating our evening meal, someone knocked on the door. We didn't usually have many visitors, so we couldn't imagine who was coming to our house this late in the day. My father got up to go to the door. In a few minutes, he came back into the room with a nice-looking young man behind him. My father—who is usually pretty unemotional—had tears in his eyes, and his face was pale. I thought he had seen a ghost or something. He just stood there for a few minutes and looked at each of us, saying nothing. My mother asked him what was wrong. He coughed, cleared his throat, and then said quietly, "He's come home!"

We all gasped and looked at the man who had stepped up beside my father and placed his arm around his shoulder. He was tall and handsome, dressed in a simple robe and sandals, and his voice was firm but kind. He said, "I know you're all shocked to see me, but I really am your son and brother. I'm finally in my right mind, and I want you to take me back into the family. I know how hard it has been for you, but I'm fine now, and I'm ready to take my place with you. Please let me come home!"

I couldn't believe what I was seeing! I saw a stranger, but his voice was the voice of my long-lost brother. I couldn't stop staring at him. He smiled at me and said, "Esther, I know you're shocked to see me. I'm sorry for all the mean things I did to you when we were growing up, but I'm a different person now. I know it's going to take time to accept what's happened to me, but after I explain it, maybe you'll accept the miracle of my changed life. Will you let me tell you my story?"

Still in a state of near shock, we all walked slowly back to the table and sat down. My mother asked him if he wanted something to eat, but he declined, saying he'd rather tell us what had happened to him. He began slowly, seeming to process every word before he spoke. He held out his hands and rolled up the sleeves of his robe.

"Look at my hands and arms," he said. "I lived for years among the tombs in Gadara. I couldn't take care of any of my personal needs and felt desperate and alone. I started cutting myself with rocks, just like I had done as a child, and walking around the area screaming at anybody who came near. Everyone was afraid of me, and I don't blame them. Local authorities tried to take me into the village in chains, but I was able to break the chains and run away back to the caves and tombs. They even tried to bind my feet with iron clamps, but I broke them too. Eventually, they gave up on me and just let me run loose, warning everyone in the village to stay away from me. I remember all these things now, but I didn't realize what I had been doing until one special day not long ago."

"What was so special about that day?" my mother asked.

"It was miraculous," my brother answered. "This man, this rabbi—I learned later that he was a rabbi from Nazareth—walked toward me. I remember screaming at him and begging him on my knees not to torture me. Then the most unusual thing happened! He reached down and took my hand, pulled me to my feet, and said, 'Come out of this man, you evil spirit!'"

He stopped for a moment and then, catching a breath with a suggestion of a smile on his face, he tried to explain something about a crowd of pigs that started acting strangely, but none of us could quite follow that part of his story. He actually laughed when he told us about them, and then he said, "Maybe those pigs just took all the craziness out of me!" We all looked at one another in confusion, so he continued with his story.

"At that moment, I suddenly realized all that I had been doing—all that had happened to me over the years—and I felt a strange warmth all over my body. I couldn't understand it, but I almost automatically knew that I would never have to live among the tombs again! I'm finally home, if you will have me."

51

When he said this, we all joined hands and began hugging one another, for we had just seen a miracle walk through our door. There will be much more that he will want to tell us, I'm sure. We will probably spend many hours thinking about all that he will tell us, but one thing is sure. God loves us all, and this miracle worker must be his representative—maybe even his son, as was prophesied. I'm sure we will hear more about him in the future. Who knows what other miracles he has performed.

Think about It!

1. Consider the Word

Read Mark 5:1–20; Matthew 8: 28–34; Luke 8:26–39.

2. Consider Your Response

How would you describe this man? Insane? Crazy? Loony? Nuts? Off his rocker? How would you feel if someone you knew acted this way? What if this man happened to be a member of your family? Is there a treatment that is available where you live? Would you help this man try to find help? Why or why not?

Is there a spiritual lesson somewhere in this story? Are there people you know who are in spiritual confusion about what happens to them? How would you try to help that person?

(Write your responses below.)

Prayer Time: Thank God for his love for all people and his concern for our well-being. Ask him to grant more understanding and compassion for people with mental and/or spiritual confusion.

JARON

My former wife, Mirah, was a very curious woman. She was also a very beautiful and desirable woman. When I met her, she had already been married twice and was not ashamed to admit that she was looking for number three. She flirted with every man she met, whether he was married or not. She would smile—quite a seductive smile, I might add—and toss her hair around her shoulders, all the while looking directly into your eyes. Those eyes spoke volumes about her intent to try to seduce every male she met. I have to admit that I wanted her when I first met her. I'm not sure whether it was love, desire, or just plain curiosity, but whatever it was, I was hooked.

We moved in together, and for the first few months, everything was fine. But, as you might expect, she began her, shall we say, *inviting* ways whenever we went anywhere together. It wasn't long before I realized the inevitable—that she was tired of me and was looking for another man to seduce. I finally decided to leave a few years ago, but I still saw her around town occasionally, always with a man. I heard recently that she had married twice after I left and that she was now living with someone she had not married.

Now, here's where the real story begins. People are friendly here because Sychar is not that big of a town. It's the kind of town where people know each other and get along without too many problems. These friends that I have known most of my life love to get together to, shall we say, share information about others. They tell me about what they have heard about Mirah, and some of the stories are pretty outrageous. But there's one incident that is really hard to believe, although I know it has to be true.

My friends talk a lot, but I have never known them to deliberately lie or make up stories about anybody in town. When they told me about what happened to Mirah, it was really hard to believe, because, after all, I was married to her for over a year, and I couldn't even begin to understand what happened to her.

The story says that she was down at the city well drawing water in the middle of the day, around noon, I think they said. That was curious, because most of the people go for water in late afternoon because of the daytime heat. The women who usually went to draw water would talk about her, push her out of the way, call her names, and ignore her when she tried to talk to them, so she decided to go to the well when she could be alone and not have to endure the taunts of the other women of the town.

On this particular day—and the story is that she has shared the incident with many people—she was at the well when this traveling rabbi stopped, sat down on the side of the well, and asked her for a drink of water. That was very unusual, because most men wouldn't even think of asking a woman for water. It was so unusual that Mirah struck up a conversation with this rabbi, asking him questions and trying to find out more about him and why he was in our town. This was not unusual for Mirah. She has always been curious, as I have said, and she can start a conversation with anybody who is willing to listen to her. She even told some of the men in town that she asked him lots of questions, trying to find out what he had in mind for her. As I understand it, she even questioned him about Jacob's well, as the townspeople named it, and how and where people should worship. She even questioned him about the promise of a Messiah that she had heard about. According to the information that the men heard from her, she said that she had heard that this promised Messiah would reveal himself to people and tell them the secrets of their lives. When she said that, this stranger, this rabbi, this friendly visitor, this man who talks to women beside the well said that he was that Messiah! Can you believe that? Then, and I don't believe this part of the story, she said he told her all about her life—her husbands and the man she was living with now. That's incredible! Everyone in town knows that, but how did this stranger know? He had not been here before, and certainly she had never seen him anywhere before. Why would the holy Promised One from God stop beside a well to talk to a woman like her? Why would he ask her for a drink of water? I'm having trouble believing all this. So I asked some of my other friends around town what they thought about Mirah's story. I was rather surprised at what I learned.

My friends said that the rabbi and his traveling companions—I heard there were probably twelve men who traveled with him—gathered together in town, and he began teaching the crowds who had gathered. He was telling them about God, his blessings, his promises, and the Messiah—God's Son—who would come to the earth to lead people to God. The crowds grew larger as he talked, and they invited him to stay for two more days. This rabbi and his companions stayed. Many of my friends went to hear him speak, and they became convinced that he really was the Promised One from God! I understand that some of them told Mirah that they believed in him as the Messiah after they heard him speak, and they gave her credit for introducing him to them.

It's quite remarkable that this woman could have been the instrument that directed so many people to the one true God. I guess I should be thankful that she was at least a small part of my life. If he can change her—if he can convince so many of my friends that he is the one sent from God, that he is truly the Messiah—it must be true. I'm going to try to find out where he is going to be and make an effort to meet him personally. I could use a good change in my life! He sounds like the one who can do that for me!

Think about It!

1. Consider the Word

Read John 4:4–30.

2. Consider Your Response

Have you ever known a woman like this Samaritan woman? If so, how did you feel about her lifestyle? If not, how do you think you would react if someone introduced her to you? Would you be friendly? Would you turn away? Would you think of names she should be called? Would you tell others about meeting her?

How would you react if a member of your family had this kind of a reputation? Why do you think Jesus reacted to her the way he did? He obviously knew about her before he spoke to her. Is there an example here for us to follow?

(Write your responses below.)

Prayer Time: Thank God for his forgiving love. Ask him to give you more love and compassion for people who live their lives differently from yours.

MIRIAM

Bethany has always been a good town. People help one another and look out for anything that seems to be unusual. We care for the sick, grieve for the lost, and rejoice with the newborns. We are all neighbors, friends, and helpers to one another.

My situation, however, is a little unusual. My neighbors next door have a strange family relationship. There are two sisters and a brother who live together. None of them are married, and they stay pretty much to themselves. The women, Mary and her sister, Martha, will talk with those of us at the well when we all gather water for the day, but when they are at home, they don't get outside very much. Martha, I understand, is quite a good cook and seems to be the one who runs the household. Someone told me that Mary, the quiet one, actually wanted to learn to read! I can't imagine what for. None of the other women I know ever considered learning to read. It wouldn't matter much anyway. The men rule the town and the synagogue. They would consider a woman who reads as being too uppity.

The family does have guests frequently though. There is one particular visitor who shows up every now and then to have a meal with them, usually bringing several men with him. Someone told me that he was a rabbi, and the men with him were his students. I didn't know his name until recently, but he visits quite often, and the women seem to look forward to his coming.

The brother, Lazarus, is a hard worker. He leaves early in the morning and comes back home late in the afternoon. I'm not sure what he does, but when I see him, he looks tired.

Several weeks ago, some strange events took place. I can't quite understand all that happened, but it's still the talk of the town. Lazarus was taken ill. I don't know what caused it, but he was really very sick. I went over to take some food to the family and to offer any help they might need, but Martha said everything was under control. She thanked me for the food but didn't invite me in. Then, just a few days later, we got word that Lazarus had died. Most of the village was at his funeral, of course. I joined in with the other women for the grief procession to the grave site. Mary and Martha were devastated and could hardly bear the thought of losing their brother, their protector, their mainstay in the home. Many of the villagers tried to express their condolences to the women, but they were beside themselves with grief. They seemed at a loss as to what to do.

At the village well the next morning, one of their closer neighbors told me that the women tried to get in touch with their rabbi friend, but he hadn't shown up while Lazarus was sick. Then, after he died, they sent for their friend again. When he finally came after Lazarus had been dead for four days, Martha was really angry with him for not coming earlier. She even scolded him for not coming and said that if the rabbi had not neglected them, Lazarus wouldn't have died.

Now the story gets really interesting! Here's what I learned from others in the village. The rabbi, whose name I finally learned was Jesus—he was from the town of Nazareth, I think—went to the house and asked where Lazarus was buried. When the women took him to the tomb, this rabbi broke down and wept! I can't imagine that happening. Men don't cry, especially rabbis. They are always so stoic about everything and don't show much emotion, but everyone who was around said that it was true. Then—and this is *really* hard to believe—the rabbi told everyone to stand back. He called out in a loud voice, "Lazarus, come forth!" I don't know if the people who told me this were hallucinating, in shock, or what, but they said they saw Lazarus walk out of the grave alive! Some of the men even got close enough to him to unravel his burial clothes!

Now, we all know that dead people can't come back from the grave. That's just impossible. At least that's what I thought until I looked out my front door yesterday and, lo and behold! There was Lazarus in front of his house, greeting people who had come to see if what they had heard was really true! I had to get a closer look, so I walked over to join the crowd and saw him up close. It really was Lazarus, my neighbor, talking to the people! His sisters, Mary and Martha, were standing with him, explaining that it was this rabbi, Jesus, who had raised their brother from the dead. They were so excited! It was a great miracle that had happened, and they couldn't explain it. All they knew was that their brother was back with them again.

Now, I went to Lazarus's funeral; I watched the family bury him; I watched his sisters greet people from the village who came to pay their respects; I heard about their intense grief; and I saw Lazarus himself yesterday! I even began to doubt my own sanity! If what I have heard about this Jesus is true, and I have no reason to doubt it, I'm going to try to find out more about him. I have a cousin who lives in Nazareth, and as soon as I can find the time, I'm going to try to visit her and learn more about this man. I want to know who he really is, how he can do what he did, and where I can go to find him. There are some of my own people who have died that I would like to see again.

I wonder. Could it be that this man really is the Jewish Messiah I have heard so much about? My father used to tell me stories about how the old prophets had spoken of a great one to come from God who would change the world and provide healing for the sick and life for the dead. He would tell me about how the priests in the synagogue would read from prophets like Isaiah about the one who was to come to save his people, Israel. His eyes would have a faraway look as he spoke of the hope of this coming Savior. Could this Jesus be the one? If he is, I want to know more about him, and I'm going to do everything I can to find out what I can! Maybe I can find him and invite him to my home for a meal. I wouldn't even mind preparing enough for those students of his who follow him wherever he goes! Let's see. What do I do first? Maybe I'll just take some food to these neighbors and see if I can get them to tell me more about what happened that day. It should be quite a story!

THINK ABOUT IT !

1. Consider the Word:

Read John 11:1–44; 12:1–10.

2. Consider Your Response

Grief comes to most everyone during a lifetime. Most of us have experienced the loss of someone we love—a family member, a friend, a coworker, a close neighbor. What is our usual response? Most of us share our feelings with those who are closest to us. But do we call on Jesus for comfort? Do we ask him to restore that person to life? Do we blame him for our loss? Do we question why we have to suffer? Think of someone with whom you could share personal grief or loss. Write that person's name below. Thank God for someone on whom you can call in the time of your greatest need. (Did you write Jesus's name?)

(Write Jesus a personal thank-you note for his love and care.)

Prayer Time: Thank God that he will never leave us or forsake us. Read Joshua 1:5 and say a special thanks for the Word of God, which records and testifies to his care.

HAMAN

My brother Simon has gotten involved in a very serious situation, and I'm worried about what he says happened to cause him to be so disturbed. For a long time, he had been curious about this rabbi who was traveling around the country with a group of followers, telling people about God in a way that people hadn't heard before. People said that this teacher had some sort of miraculous power that could cause people to be healed or to confess their disturbing behavior or even—and this is strange—to be raised from the dead! Now, I'm just as interested as anyone in these stories because, of course, most of them are probably just created by gullible people who want to be listened to or to gain some kind notoriety. It's hard to believe some of the stories that were circulated about this unusual man. But I digress.

I was talking about my brother Simon. The people of Cyrene know him as an honest, hardworking family man, but lately he has slacked up in his work and has started listening to more stories about this rabbi teacher known as Jesus. When I last talked to him, he told me what had caused him so much confusion. He had joined a group of friends who were curious about Jesus and had followed them to Jerusalem, where they thought he would be teaching in the temple. He and his friends were just at the edge of the city when they met a group of soldiers who were dragging Jesus like a prisoner. Simon said that Jesus looked as if he had been beaten severely, that he had some kind of sharp, pointed crown on his head, and he was carrying a large, heavy cross. Simon knew that he must have been condemned to death by crucifixion, the horrible penalty that the Romans inflicted on people who dared to challenge anything the rulers did. Following the soldiers were loud, mocking people who were jeering at him, calling him names, and spitting at him. Along the side of the road, a group of women were following the crowd and were weeping and crying Jesus's name.

Then Simon stopped for a moment, shook his head, touched his eyes, and finally continued his story. He said that Jesus suddenly stumbled and started to bend under the weight of the cross. One of the soldiers turned around, grabbed Simon by the sleeve, and ordered him to carry that cross for the prisoner. Simon was stunned, but he knew that he dare not disobey a direct order from the soldier. So he lifted the cross, moved it to his shoulders, and began the journey to the top of the hill outside Jerusalem, the hill they called Golgotha. It was at this point in the story that Simon's voice quivered a bit. He said that what happened next was hard to put into words, so he had later gone to his home, and after a while, he wrote down what had happened to him. Then he showed me what he had written, just as he remembered it. The story was very hard to believe, but Simon explained the incident very carefully. Let me show it to you.

> When I was ordered to carry the cross, it didn't bother me. I'm strong enough. But as I got closer to the man, I began to remember his voice as he spoke to us on the hillside not long ago. I couldn't remember much of what he said, but his manner was gentle. His voice rang with authority, yet it was compassionate. He didn't seem like a criminal then, just another dreamer of great dreams. Yet here was this same man, trudging up that hill to his death. Somehow it wasn't right. I couldn't understand why I suddenly felt he was innocent after all. Carrying that cross seemed the least I could do for the man. But then, when I picked up the cross, the strangeness began. It was very heavy at first—hard, solid wood. I could hardly lift it. But as it settled on my shoulders, it seemed to get strangely lighter. It was almost as if it was not there at all. As we started up the hill—and this was the strangest thing of all—he reached out and touched my arm. I turned to him and looked into his face for the first time. Never have I seen

such a face as that! Dried blood was caked on his forehead; the spit of the crowd was still on his cheeks and beard; fresh blood ran from the thorns they had pushed onto his head. But his eyes—his eyes! There was such gentleness, such tenderness, such—such love! I've never seen anything like it! Then he spoke—just three words, but his voice still had the strange combination of authority and gentleness that I remember; it was unusually strong for one in such pain. He looked me directly in the eyes and said, "Thank you, Simon." His touch was like a shock wave through my body. But—and this really shocked me: he spoke my name! How did he know my name? I had never met the man until that minute! I'm still trying to figure it all out.

When I finished reading, I waited for Simon to continue his story. I asked him to tell me what happened next. He looked up at me and then began to describe what had happened next. He said that he placed the cross on the ground at the direction of the soldier. Two other crosses were already being put into place, and the cross that Simon carried was placed between the other two. He didn't want to stay and watch what he knew was going to be a terrible scene, but he and the others were almost hypnotized by what they saw and heard. To Simon, it was a horrible, discouraging event, but he was able to hear what Jesus said while he was hanging there on that terrible cross. He said that the man forgave the ones who had been ordered to execute him. His last cry was "It is finished."

As he was telling me his story, Simon's voice grew softer. His voice shook as he told me what he had heard and seen there on that hill. Then, as he turned to leave, he looked back at me, and I could see tears in his eyes. His voice quivered as he spoke. He said, "Haman, I've never experienced anything like this before. I've always been able to control events in my life. But this was different. I don't know much about any religion or what people believe about their God or any so-called Messiah. But one thing I do know. Something happened to me that day. And I'll never be the same again!"

As he walked away, his step was slow, his shoulders were hunched over, and he seemed to be wiping his eyes. Then he stopped, looked back at me, waved and smiled, and started back to his home.

I've been thinking a lot about his story. It doesn't make a lot of sense to me, but, as I said, I've never known Simon to make up stories, especially one as hard to believe as this one. I'm going to have to think a lot about what he told me. I think I may have to look up some of the people who witnessed the outcome of this story. Anything as unusual as this incident must have made a strong impression on the bystanders around the crucifixion scene. Maybe I'll find out more about all this soon. I hope so. I still have to work it all out in my mind. There's more to the story, I'm sure. I'm anxious to hear what others have to say. It should be very interesting!

THINK ABOUT IT!

1. Consider the Word

Read Matthew 27:32–40; Mark 15:20–22; Luke 23:26–43.

2. Consider Your Response

When you lift something heavy, what do you think about? *Will this hurt my back? I hope I don't drop this? I hope (name) will appreciate this? Couldn't this have been put in a smaller package? I hope I don't have to do this again?* Take a moment to remember a time you had to carry a large package or heavy load of some kind. For whom did you carry it? Did that person appreciate it? How did that make you feel? Did you volunteer or were you asked to carry it? Put yourself in Simon's place, if you can imagine the situation. How do you feel about the way the story was developed in the Bible? What spiritual message can you glean from the incident?

(Write your responses below.)

Prayer Time: Thank God for Jesus's sacrifice for you on the cross. Ask him to help you understand more clearly what he did for you and to help you to share the story with those who may not know him as Savior.

NAZOR

I've always been proud of my son, Julius. From the time he was a little boy, he had always wanted to be a soldier. He would gather the neighborhood boys around and march them up and down the street, barking out commands like a real military officer. The boys seemed to want to follow him, and when they "went to war," they would aim carefully to make sure their spears didn't hit anyone. Sometimes when they practiced hitting targets, though, he always found the mark. He seemed to delight in outscoring the others in accuracy.

As he grew older, he talked more and more about joining the army. All the young men in the city were required to spend at least three years serving the country, and he was excited when the time came for him to report to headquarters. When the day came for him to enlist, I went with him to be sure he did all the right things. He was so proud that day! When he finally got his orders and his uniform, he looked like quite a man. Both his mother and I expressed our pleasure and pride as we escorted him just to the end of our property. Real soldiers don't bring their mom and dad with them when they leave home! He made sure that we understood that!

As time went by, we wondered how he was doing. Occasionally, one of his friends would drop by to see us and tell us about Julius. We learned that he had become quite a fierce fighter in his regiment and had won several commendations from his superiors. Our expectations were not diminished; he had become the true soldier he had always wanted to be.

Not long ago—I don't remember exactly when—we learned that he had been promoted to captain of the centurion regiment that was stationed in Jerusalem. There had been several uprisings among the people there, and soldiers had to control the crowds to maintain order. Some kind of new religion was being practiced there, and lots of people were following a Jewish leader from the Galilee region. Authorities expressed concern that the people were transferring their allegiance from the government to this new rabble-rouser. Julius had been placed in charge of one of the elite execution squads. This was a popular assignment, because these squads were honored as protectors and looked upon as heroes. Besides, their salary was much larger than that of the regular soldiers on patrol.

Then, just a few days ago, Julius came home on leave. I hardly knew the boy. He had changed from the proud, strapping young man we had sent off to serve his country. He looked haggard and tired. His eyes stared blankly at us, as if he didn't even recognize his own family. He was withdrawn, quiet, and didn't want to talk to us at first. We thought he was sick, but he assured us that his health was perfectly fine. Yet he seemed troubled and just wanted to be left alone.

He stayed in that condition for several days, until one morning when he came to breakfast and asked a strange question: "Father, is there an eternity?" I was stunned! I couldn't imagine where the question had come from or how he thought I might have an answer. I replied that it was a question I couldn't answer. I had never thought about it. Then I asked him why he would ask such a question.

Then began a very strange story of an unusual execution to which he had been a witness. He did not participate in the actual execution but had been directed to make the assignments to the rest of the squad to keep the crowds of mourners away from the scene. He said that many were screaming and crying and cursing the Romans for their brutal punishment of anyone who dared to protest against their rule or to cause any disturbance in the city. He had to constantly patrol the area to be sure the crowds were under control. He told us about the man whom the soldiers in his squad had crucified weeks earlier, the young Jewish leader who had been causing so much concern to the government officials. He said that he had heard that even the Jewish leaders condemned him for teaching strange ideas foreign to their beliefs. These Jewish leaders had demanded that the one they called Jesus be put to death for inciting an insurrection and for blasphemy against the Jewish faith. They even claimed that he said that he was God!

Of course I was interested in the story, for we, too, had heard of this leader and what he was teaching as he traveled around the country. His fame had reached across almost every territory. People claimed that he healed sick people, and one woman from Bethany even claimed that he had raised one of her neighbors from the dead! Naturally, I didn't believe that tall tale, but it made for interesting conversation.

Julius went on to tell us about the man. He said that while he was on the cross, this Jesus refused to curse and scream like others he had seen executed. Instead, he was quiet in his suffering, just an occasional deep breath and moaning. He even spoke to the people who were standing there watching him die. He asked for some water, because he was thirsty; he said something to one of the others there on the cross next to him. Julius couldn't hear what he said to the man. But the statement that hit our son so hard was when that so-called criminal on the cross cried out, "Father, forgive them, for they don't know what they are doing!" He begged his God to forgive the people who were putting him to death!

"That included me," Julius said. "No one has ever said anything like that during an execution! Even though I don't actually participate in executions, I have to stand by and try to maintain some kind of order. Usually our whole squad is cursed and told how much we are hated. Father, I'm beginning to think that man was innocent. I even made the statement that he must be the Son of God, the one these Hebrews claim as their savior. I don't know why I said it. It just seemed to be true at the time. Now I'm confused. I don't want to quit being a soldier. I don't want to be punished for leaving the regiment, but I don't think I can continue with guarding these executions. I haven't been able to sleep peacefully since that day I heard those words from the man called Jesus. What am I to do?"

I thought about what my son had said for a while before I gave him an answer. I'm not certain that my response made any sense to him, but I spoke what I thought. I told him that I had heard of the man, that stories about him had been spread about, that many people now accepted him as the Son of God, and that there were rumors that he had even risen from the dead. We heard that he had appeared in a number of places and had been seen by many people just within days of the crucifixion. It seemed very hard to believe, but reports had come from very reliable sources. I explained that, even though the information seemed factual, it was hard for me to accept that anyone could rise from the dead. However, one of our friends, the owner of a fishing boat, told us that the disciple Peter and some of Jesus's followers decided to go fishing shortly after the reports of his death. Peter's boat was docked next to our friend. He said that there had been a disturbance on the water a few minutes after Peter cast off. When the men came back to shore, they were saying that it was Jesus out on the water, and Peter had jumped in to swim to him. As our friend watched, the men ran down the beach to a campfire someone had made. There was an unusual glow around the campfire, and as they neared the spot, they smelled fish cooking over the fire. Moving closer, they drew back, startled. Telling the story later, they swore that it was Jesus—the same one who had been crucified!

I didn't know how to take this news. No one, I mean *no one*, can come back to life after they have been pronounced dead and even, in this case, buried. Yet our friend said that he could not convince Peter that it could not have been Jesus.

As for Julius, he was never the same again. After those few days at home with us, he went back to his regiment and asked to be transferred from the execution squad. The officers agreed, but they sent him to an outpost near the sea where he could "rethink his decision," as they declared.

Yesterday afternoon, a fellow soldier with Julius's regiment came home on furlough and brought this letter from our son. Let me read it to you:

Father,

I have made my final decision concerning the discussion we had when I was home. I now believe that this man whose execution I watched that day was truly the Son of the living God. My superiors have labeled me as "mad" and dismissed me from any further service obligations. They could have executed me as a traitor, I know, but somehow all they did was revoke any privileges I had as a soldier and order me never to enter Jerusalem again. I am now in the region of Galilee and intend to stay here for a while. My friend Cassio, who brings this letter, was visiting his family here and agreed to contact you for me. I have met some other believers here, and they have been very kind to me.

This man, Jesus, seems to have influenced many people in his short time around here. I will remain here and try to find some means of labor to repay the friends who have helped me so far. I have been visiting the Jewish synagogue with these friends and have learned much about them and their beliefs.

I thank you for all you have done for me. I hope I haven't disgraced you. Please give my regards to my mother and brothers. I probably will not be seeing you again, but know that I am truly happy and believe that I have found the person these Jews call their Messiah.

Your son,

Julius

I reread his letter often, just to remind me of his reasons for his decision to leave the army. I can sympathize with his feelings because I, too, have done some serious rethinking of the whole situation. This man, Jesus, seems to have touched so many lives while he was traveling and teaching.

He affected so many lives directly and indirectly, like mine. I still don't exactly know what to believe, but I am certain that he was committed to helping people know more about his God—committed enough to suffer the kind of death he was forced to experience. If he really was the Son of God—if he really was the Jewish Messiah, if he really was the Promised One, as they call him—I'm sure we will hear more about him. My son has left me with a lot to think about. I hope that he will come back home soon, even though he said he wouldn't see us again. I won't give up hope on that!

THINK ABOUT IT!

1. Consider the Word

Read Luke 23:27–49; Matthew 27:27–32; Mark 15:20–21.

2. Consider Your Response

Has anyone ever told you a story that was difficult for you to accept as truth? How did you respond? If this has never been your experience, think of a newspaper or magazine article that defied a simple explanation. What about a report on the evening news? How easily do you accept fantastic stories? Do you ever question them? Why or why not?

What if a trusted friend or family member shares an unbelievable experience with you? How easily would you accept their report? What about the messages given to us in the Bible? Do you accept them as truth? Why or why not?

(Write your responses below.)

Prayer Time: Thank God for the truth of his Word. Ask him to help you understand the truth of his messages to us.

CLAUDIUS

Our son, Teman, has always wanted to be a soldier. He liked the idea of the uniforms and the weapons and the company of others serving their country. However, I think it was the uniform that he liked the most. We tried to talk him out of joining the army, but when he reached the recruitment age, he proudly enlisted and was immediately sent to Rome for training. We hoped that this adventure would encourage him to help others and learn the importance of reaching out to people who need someone to care for them. He has always been an obedient child and has grown into an honest, dependable young man. We are very proud of him and hope that others will recognize those positive qualities in him as he serves his country. He knows how to listen and communicate with others, so his time serving his country should be a time of growing, maturing, and establishing himself as a competent, reliable, and industrious adult.

After his first few months in the army, we learned from another soldier's parents that Teman had been assigned to a special group in Jerusalem. We had heard about some of the problems that Rome was having in that city. It seems that there had been some trouble in that area because of a teacher who had attracted large crowds of people to hear him. His teachings were considered quite radical, they said, and the teacher had been arrested and put on trial. Pilate—I think that was the name of the governor—tried to keep the prisoner from the death penalty for disturbing the area, but the crowd didn't listen to him and demanded that the teacher be crucified for causing so much trouble. After trying to change the mind of the crowd, the governor just gave up and turned him over to the soldiers for execution.

We were very concerned about Teman and his role in this situation, but our friends said that their son, who had come home after serving his time in the army, told them that Teman had been assigned to keep watch at the prisoner's grave site so that his body would not be disturbed by his followers. It seems that the people who followed this man's teaching believed that he would somehow come back to life, and his enemies didn't want some of his believers to try to steal his body, so Pilate ordered Teman and another soldier to stand guard all night. This seemed to be quite an honor for these two young soldiers, and we were told that both of them felt proud that they had been chosen for this duty. Of course, we were very proud of our son, and we knew that he would do his job faithfully.

It wasn't until a few months later that we heard the rest of the story. Teman was allowed to return home for a visit, and we were very excited that he was allowed to stay at home for a while. We didn't really know the circumstances of his visit, but we were so pleased when he finally got home, and we were able to see what a difference his time in the army had made. The difference in our son was very noticeable. He wasn't the exuberant young man we had seen when he enlisted. He was quieter, more subdued, more thoughtful, and not quite as easy to talk to. We just thought that his behavior and his demeanor were attributed to his maturing, but we soon learned that there was much more to explain what had happened to him.

He didn't talk much for the first few days, but we finally persuaded him to sit down and tell us what had happened. We knew that something had caused the changes in our son, so we persuaded him to tell us what had happened. He hesitated at first and said that we probably wouldn't believe him; his superiors didn't, and they had tried to get him to change his story. They had even paid him extra money to lie about what he had heard and seen after the execution of that prisoner. Teman was always an honest boy, and we could always depend on him to tell the truth. We were proud that we had never found him to tell anything but the truth, but when his superior officers ordered him to lie about that particular night after the execution and say that he was asleep, he was reluctant and tried to get the officer to believe what he and the other soldier had seen. His companion that night, another soldier who had been appointed to guard the tomb—I think his name was Ethan—didn't seem to mind lying about what had happened, especially since they were given a large sum of money to deny what had happened. Actually, Ethan was telling the truth about the situation. He really was asleep and only woke up when all the excitement began. It took a while for Teman to finish his story, but we waited patiently to hear what had happened.

It seems that Teman and Ethan were watching the people come and go around the burial site. The prisoner—the teacher who had been crucified, that Roman order to punish offenders—had been buried in a small cave, and a large rock had been placed at the entrance. The two young men were ordered to keep special watch because the teacher's followers believed that he really was going to rise from the dead. Our son didn't believe such a story, and neither did Ethan, but they took their responsibilities seriously and kept a close watch.

Now, here's where the story gets interesting. The men took turns sleeping on the first night of their watch, but on the second night, very early in the morning while Ethan was still asleep, several women came to the tomb. It was unusual for women to be around any burial place, but our son thought that they must be some of the followers of this rabbi. There had been rumors that several women had traveled with him as he moved through the area preaching his message. As the women gathered around the entrance, the ground started shaking, the trees around them started to fall, there was loud thunder, and the ground began to break apart at their feet. Ethan woke up shouting, and they both tried to brace themselves against one of the large rocks in the area. A brilliant light blinded them both for a minute, but when they regained their eyesight, they saw what they said was a figure like an angel who moved slowly toward the rock that blocked the entrance to that special tomb. The figure touched the rock that blocked the door, and suddenly, with a great rumble, the stone rolled away!

As he told the story, Teman stopped to catch his breath. He shook his head, paused for a moment, and looked up at us. I could see that his eyes were wet with tears. This was so unlike him. My wife and I didn't say anything. We just looked at each other and then waited for him to continue his story of that unbelievable night.

The angel figure was brilliant with light and was covered in a white garment of some kind. The young men were so frightened that they tried to hide behind one of the big rocks close by. They could see what was happening, and they were terrified. Teman paused here to catch his breath, looked up at us, and then turned his head for a moment. Then he said that the angel figure spoke with a beautiful, comforting voice and told the women that the prisoner had actually risen from the dead! The angel said that the women should go and tell the followers of the teacher that he would meet them later. The women left quickly. There was a brilliant light that blinded the men, and when they regained their sight, the figure was gone, and the women had left. There was no sign of anyone around the tomb—no people, no sound, no bright light. Instead, there was a strange and rather uncomfortable stillness in the air. Their curiosity about what they had seen prompted Teman and Ethan to look inside the tomb. They moved carefully toward the entrance and slowly stepped just inside. To their amazement, they saw the burial cloth and the head covering lying on the ground, the headpiece just above the body cloth. Looking at each other in disbelief, they decided that they should report what they had seen so that they would not be punished for letting the tomb be opened.

The young men went to the headquarters in the city and told their superiors what had happened. Of course, they were questioned about every detail, but when the story was finished and they made no changes, their commanding officer told them not to tell anyone else what had happened. They were given two months' salary and told to say that the followers of the teacher had come in the night while they were asleep and had stolen the teacher's body! Now, it was a well-known fact that no soldier has ever gotten away from serious punishment for sleeping on duty, and Teman didn't want to tell a lie about it, so he was told to return home for a while to think about what had happened that night. Of course, his partner could follow instructions because he actually was asleep when this happened.

After our son finished his story, we waited for a few minutes to gather our thoughts. My wife and I agreed that our son had done the right thing in refusing to deny what had happened. We are convinced that he was telling the truth. We have never had any reason to doubt him, and, actually, what he told us made sense to us. We had heard stories about this man, Jesus, and his miracle works. We now had a sense of being very honored that our son had been present at that very special place, on that very special night, to witness that very special miracle.

The events that our son has experienced have changed him—and us. He told us that he now believes that this prisoner whose grave he had been assigned to guard was really the chosen one that the Hebrew people believed would come to deliver them from their oppression. There have been many stories about what this man has done. Perhaps the stories we have heard about this miracle worker are really true. Maybe he really was—is—the Messiah these Hebrews have been taught would appear. We are curious to know more about those promises. Because of the story that our son told us, that this crucified prisoner really did rise from his tomb, we believe we may hear more about him in the future! There probably are countless others who will be hearing about this for many years to come. An event like this can't be kept secret for very long. Others are bound to tell the story. Maybe someone will write the story, and it will be read by people in the future. Who knows what might happen. I only know that our son has given us something to think about for a long time. I don't think we'll ever be the same again after hearing about this!

Think about It!

1. Consider the Word

Read Matthew 27:62–28:15.

2. Consider Your Response

Think of a time when someone told you an unbelievable story. How did you react? Have you read about some incident that made no sense to you? How did you react? What did you think about the person who told you the story or who wrote about it? Could you think of some reasonable explanation? Did you share it with anyone? Have you ever embellished the telling of an incident in your life in order for people to believe you? Why? Can you identify with storytellers who add imaginative details to an actual incident?

How do you respond to the stories that you have read in the Bible? Has anything about the resurrection story affected your decision about accepting Christ as your Savior? If you are a Christian, share your story. If not, why not reread what Christ has done for you? Your life—and your future—will be changed for the better. That's a promise!

(Write your responses below.)

Prayer Time: Thank God for sending Jesus to save you, and thank him for his willingness to make that sacrifice for you. Ask him to give you the desire to share this message to others who may not know him.

DOTHAN

My cousin Cleopas told me a strange story—indeed an unbelievable story—the other day. He's always been curious about events around town and tries to find out the sources of stories people tell. Oh, the stories he tells are true—no falsehoods at all. He just loves to involve people in conversation and get their opinion on what he says. He is well-known in Emmaus, our little village near Jerusalem, and his account of what happened to him seems to be true, but it's still very hard to comprehend. People all over town are still amazed at his story, and many of them have asked him questions about what he says he saw. They are continuously bothering him to retell his story. I don't think a lot of them believe him. I think they might be trying to catch him in a falsehood. It really is a strange story, but Cleopas vows that it is true.

Now, as I said, Cleopas is a curious person. He's not like a gossip or anyone who wants to be the center of attention, nothing like that. He just likes people; he's very sociable, and people like to be around him. He has lots of friends, and sometimes he and a friend will walk for miles just to hear someone tell a story or explain an adventure they have experienced. Lately, he's been traveling with a group who was following a young rabbi from Nazareth. People say this rabbi was a popular speaker and always drew a crowd wherever he went. Cleopas had shared with me some of the teachings of this man, and I have always been curious about the sources of his teachings. Cleopas really believes he is some kind of special messenger sent from God.

There had been rumors that the local Pharisees considered this teacher as a problem to their ministry and that they were looking for excuses to get rid of him somehow. Several of the leaders, I understand, actually wanted him to be arrested and brought to trial for disturbing the peace. Cleopas said he had heard that the situation was getting more serious, and when the rabbi—I think they said his name was Jesus—came to Jerusalem, the Pharisees were plotting to stop him no matter what they had to do. So Cleopas and one of his close friends decided to travel to Jerusalem to try to find out more about the plot.

Well now, back to Cleopas and the unusual part of his story. He and his friend had been in Jerusalem and heard from the witnesses of the arrest and trial, such as it was. They had watched at a distance as the Roman soldiers crucified the rabbi, along with two other condemned men. After the convicted prisoners had been pronounced dead and removed from those awful crosses, Cleopas suggested that the two of them return to Emmaus. They were devastated by what they had seen. Both of them felt sick about what had happened to the man they had been so curious about, so they decided to stay in Jerusalem for a couple of days just to recuperate from what they had witnessed before they started to walk home.

Now, here's where the story really gets interesting. While they were walking along the road toward home, a stranger caught up with them and started a conversation. He seemed to be curious about what had happened in Jerusalem, and Cleopas tried to explain the story to the stranger. The stranger asked very penetrating questions and pushed Cleopas for a detailed explanation of what he had seen and heard. Cleopas told the stranger what they had witnessed and how it had affected him and his friend. The stranger was very attentive and listened carefully to the story.

When they got to his house, Cleopas invited his friend and the stranger to come in for a meal. And here's where the story takes another remarkable turn. When they sat down to eat, this stranger thanked Cleopas for his invitation. Before they began to eat, he bowed his head, reached his hands over the table, and started to bless the food. Suddenly, Cleopas recognized the voice he had heard so many times before at those gatherings, that authoritative voice that spoke for God. He said that he immediately knew, without any doubt, that this had to be the rabbi—this Jesus—whom they had seen put to death by that Roman execution squad! I couldn't believe what he was telling me. Nobody, I mean *nobody*, can come back to life after they're pronounced dead, no matter who makes up the story. I thought at first that it was just another incident that had somehow caught the attention of my guests, but then Cleopas added another part to the story. After the stranger had blessed the food and the wine, he just vanished before their eyes! I caught my breath for a moment and asked if anyone else had witnessed what they said they had seen. Of course, no one else was at the dinner table except Cleopas and his friend. They both seemed rather in a state of shock at remembering what they had experienced. His friend still seemed unable to grasp the reality of the situation but swore that Cleopas was telling the truth.

Now, Cleopas, as I said, is well-known for listening to and repeating village stories, but this one was different. I've never seen him so excited or so convinced of the reality of what he had experienced. And his friend verified every detail of the story! We talked a little while longer about some of the things we had heard about this man. He had been described as a miracle worker, a compassionate friend, an almost mesmerizing speaker, and, some said, the Messiah that had been promised by the prophets. The two friends didn't seem to reach any definitive conclusions; they agreed on the details but couldn't explain how it all happened. Those of us who heard their story were still questioning how they could have seen what they claimed they saw.

I heard later that Cleopas and his friend—I don't remember his name—went to Bethany, where devoted followers of this Jesus had gone to hear him, this resurrected miracle worker. The story is that, while they were there, while they watched and listened, he began to glow like the sun and actually rose to heaven in their sight! And I understand that others who were there also confirmed the experience, and many of them decided to share the story with everyone they met. Some even committed to organizing groups to meet regularly to share their beliefs and to pray for others to join them.

I still haven't figured it all out. As I have said, Cleopas doesn't lie. Others in the village confirm the honesty of the friend who also witnessed these events. I have no reason to doubt their story because of the reaction of the crowd who also witnessed the event. There are many people in the village who have confirmed the report. But it's really hard to understand and completely believe what they said. I think I'll go over to Bethany soon to visit my brother and his family. Someone told me that they had gotten curious about this Jesus and had been to hear him speak on a couple of occasions. Maybe they can help me fill in the gaps of this remarkable story. Maybe they were even in the crowd that saw him disappear bodily. Maybe I'll finally be convinced that this Jesus really was the Promised One from God! I'd really like to believe that!

Think about It!

1. Consider the Word

Read Luke 24:13–50; Mark 16:12–13.

2. Consider Your Response

Did you enjoy hearing fairy tales when you were a child? Did you think they were really true? Do you hear stories from others today that you have trouble believing? Do you accuse them of lying or exaggerating the facts? How do you respond to a really unbelievable story? How did you respond when you first heard about Jesus and the miracles he performed? How did you react to the story of his crucifixion and resurrection when you first heard it? Do you believe all the details about these events now? Why or why not?

If you are a true believer, how would you explain Jesus's miracles and his crucifixion and resurrection to a nonbeliever? Have you ever tried? Why or why not?

(Write your responses below.)

Prayer Time: Thank God for his plan of salvation for you—his crucifixion and resurrection. Ask him to help you be a better witness of his great sacrificial love for all.

A BACKWARD LOOK

Just to help us examine our own thoughts about Jesus, let's take another look at some of the stories you have read. Try to match each statement found in one of the stories. Then take a moment to examine your own thoughts about this Jesus you have read about. When you have finished checking your recollection, write your own testimony in the space provided at the closing of the pages.

Match the number of the title character's name to where the testimony is found. (It's okay to look back!)

(Characters are in alphabetical order to help you.)

1. Claudius	6. Ibram	11. Miriam
2. Dothan	7. Jacob	12. Nazor
3. Esther	8. Jaron	13. Olivia
4. Ezra	9. Jotham	14. Paulus
5. Haman	10. Maria	15. Sarai

_____1. "Maybe he really *was* the Son of God!"

_____2. "Could it be that this man really is the Jewish Messiah I have heard so much about?"

_____3. "Maybe I'll finally be convinced that this Jesus really was the Promised One from God!"

_____4. "Perhaps the stories we have heard about this miracle worker are really true."

_____5. "I could use a good change in my life!"

_____6. "Could this visitor to our home really be the one we've heard so many people talk about—the Promised One?"

_____7. "This man, this rabbi—I learned later that he was a rabbi from Nazareth—walked toward me."

_____8. "I wanted to know where his power to heal came from."

_____9. "I'm a different person because of this Jesus—that was his name."

_____10. "That man, that kind teacher, actually seemed to be in touch with the God I heard about as a child."

_____11. "I know there must be some reasonable explanation for what happened."

_____12. "I think I might have to look up some of the people who witnessed the outcome of this story."

_____13. "This man, Jesus, seems to have touched so many lives while he was traveling and teaching."

_____14 "Maybe he really was who they said he was: the Promised One of God."

_____15. "My life is forever changed because of this experience, and I don't think I'll ever be the same again."

Now, after you check your answers (look at the bottom of the author page), write your own testimony in the space below:

Sign your name here: _____

ABOUT THE AUTHOR

Dorothy Harmon is a pastor's wife and former high school teacher. She has been a newspaper columnist, a writer for Lifeway (formerly the Baptist Sunday School Board), and a Bible study writer and teacher. She is the author of the following books:

Archibald Rutledge: The Man and His Books

Miracle on Main Street (a church history)

Prayer Is … (devotionals)

The Good Book of Prayer (Bible study)

Answers to "A Backward Look":

1. 6	6. 4	11. 10
2. 11	7. 3	12. 5
3. 2	8. 15	13. 12
4. 1	9. 14	14. 9
5. 8	10. 13	15. 7

Printed in the United States
By Bookmasters